100% PROFIT

JEFFREY CROCKETT

Copyright © 2021 Jeffrey Crockett
All rights reserved
First Edition

PAGE PUBLISHING, INC.
Conneaut Lake, PA

First originally published by Page Publishing 2021

ISBN 978-1-6624-4992-5 (pbk)
ISBN 978-1-6624-4993-2 (digital)

Printed in the United States of America

Buyers can start any business within this book to make fast profits. This is a great book that is already set up for business.

With purchase of book, buyer's are in the driver's seat to resale this powerful turnkey system book at what ever price they want. Businesses within 100% Profits can be sold separately for ultimate customer satisfaction. Buyer's can start any business within this book to making fast profits. This is a great book that is already set up for Business.

Now You Can Make Extra Money from Home!

Dear friend,

Would you like to earn extra money without leaving your home? Who wouldn't? With today's rising cost of living, almost every working person needs a second income. Here are three great ways to make that extra income:

Camera profits (using your camera for extra money)!

More people own cameras than radios and photography is one of the fastest-growing hobbies in the world. With a little imagination and a little sales ability, the average person can easily make an extra $300 a week with their camera.

How to make big profits in mail order starting from scratch!

Mail-order marketing is one of the fastest and easiest ways to make money in today's economy. This is a way for the average person to own a business without investing a lot of money…and best of all, you can run this business from home. All you need is a product to sell and the right market to sell it to. You will learn how to get good products to sell by mail and how to find a market for those products. Right now, there are ordinary people like you making $500 to $2,000 and more per week in their own home mail-order business.

How to start your own day care center!

Today, there is a definite need for day care centers as more and more mothers of preschool age children are forced to find jobs outside the home. Many experts predict a greater demand for day cares in the future. Now is a good time to start your own day care from home. You can make very good money operating a day care center.

How to Start a Profitable Home-Based Business

In these days, it's becoming increasingly difficult to make ends meet with just one source of income. Thus, more and more people are investigating the possibilities of starting their own extra-income businesses. Most of these part-time endeavors are started and operated from the comfort and privacy of the home. Most of these people are making the extra money they need. Some have wisely and carefully built these extra income efforts into fulltime, very profitable businesses. Others are just keeping busy, having fun, and enjoying life as never before. The important thing is that they are doing something other than waiting for the government to give them a handout; they are improving their lot in life, and you can do it too!

The fields of mail-order selling—multi-level marketing and in-home party sales—have never been more popular. If any of these kinds of extra income-producing ideas appeal to you, then you owe it to yourself to check them out. But these aren't the only fields of endeavor you can start and operate from home, with little or no investment, and learn as you go.

If you type, you can start a home-based typing service; if you have a truck or have access to a trailer, you can start a clean-up/hauling service. Simply collecting old newspapers from your neighbors can get you started in the paper recycling business. More than a few enterprising housewives have found success and fortune by starting home and/or apartment cleaning services. If you have a yard full of flowers, you can make good extra money by supplying fresh-cut flowers to restaurants and offices in your area on a regular basis. You might turn a ceramics hobby into a lucrative personalized coffee mug business. What I'm saying is that in reality, there's literally no end to the ways you can start and operate a profitable extra-income business from your home.

The first thing you must do, however, is some basic market research. Find out for yourself, first-hand, just how many people there are in your area who are interested in your proposed product or service and would be "willing to stand in line and pay money for it." This is known as defining your market and pinpointing your customers. If after checking around, talking about your idea with a whole lot of people over a period of one to three months and you get the idea that these people would be paying customers, your next effort should be directed toward the "detailing" of your business plan. The more precise and detailed your plan—covering all the bases relating to how you'll do everything that needs to be done—the easier it's going to be for you to attain success. Such a plan should show your startup investment needs, your advertising plan, your production costs and procedures, your sales program, and how your time will be allocated. Too often, enthusiastic and ambitious entrepreneurs jump in on an extra-income project and suddenly find that the costs are beyond their abilities and the time requires more than they can meet. It pays to lay it all out on paper before you get involved, and the clearer you can "see" everything before you start, the better your chances for success.

Now, assuming you've got your market targeted, you know who your customers are going to be and how you're going to reach them with your product or service. And you have all your costs as well as time requirements itemized. The next step is to set your plan in motion and start making money.

Here is the most important "secret" of all, relating to starting and building a profitable home-based business, so read very carefully. Regardless of what kind of business you start, you must have the capital and the available time to sustain your business through the first six months of operation. Specifically, you must not count on receiving or spending any money coming in from your business on yourself or for your bills during those first six months. All the income from your business during those first six months should be reinvested in your business in order for it to grow and reach your planned first-year potential. Once you've passed that first six months milestone, you can set up a small monthly salary for yourself and begin enjoying the fruits of your labor. But the first six months of operation for any business are critical, so do not plan to use any of the money your business generates for yourself during that period.

If you've got your business plan properly organized and have implemented the plan, you should at the end of your first year be able to begin thinking about hiring other people to alleviate some of your workload. Remember this: Starting a successful business is not a means toward either a job for yourself or a way to keep busy, it should be regarded as the beginning of an enterprise that will grow and prosper with you as the top dog. Eventually, you'll have other people doing all the work for you, even running the entire operation, while you vacation in the Bahamas or Hawaii and collect or receive regular income from your initial efforts.

CAMERA PROFITS USING YOUR CAMERA FOR EXTRA MONEY

Camera Profits Using Your Camera for Extra Money

One of the easiest ways of making extra money is with a camera. More people own cameras than radios and photography is the fastest-growing hobby in the world. Yet using a camera as an extra income tool is largely overlooked!

With a little imagination, a flair for showmanship, and just a hint of salesmanship, the average man or woman or even teenager can easily make an extra $300 a week with his camera. You don't have to have one of the popular, more expensive cameras either or a loot of high-priced attachments and equipment. In many instances, a Polaroid or other "off-the-wall" camera will suit the purposes perfectly. The only special piece of extra equipment you may want to invest in would be a tripod for mounting the camera in certain situations.

One of the easiest ideas is to visit a children's clothing store in one of your busy shopping centers or the children's department in one of your large department stores. Sell the manager or store owner on the idea of your setting up in a corner of the store or department and taking pictures of the shoppers' children. He can promote the fact that you'll be in the store taking pictures for special prices during certain hours—perhaps on Friday evenings and all day Saturdays—in his advertising, thus drawing patrons into his store because of you.

You'll need a sheet or a plain piece of material or some sort of imaginative set for a background. But this you can easily make or build yourself. You should also have an eye-catching poster that calls attention to what you're doing and the prices you're charging. Unless you're a commercial artist, spend the money to have this sign made for you by a professional.

The next and last thing you'll need will be a two-part receipt or coupon. This can be a simple piece of paper of about two inches wide by S" long. On the left side, draw lines for your customers to fill in their name, telephone number, and address. You might also want to include space for additional information such as the child's name and age and the number of children in the family for future efforts but keep it brief and simple.

On the right-hand side of this coupon, have your business name, address, and telephone number, plus a quick outline of the different kinds of photography work you handle and perhaps a business slogan, such as "Satisfaction Guaranteed or You Don't Pay."

To add a little bit of class to this coupon, take the basic outline of this idea over to an instant print shop. Tell them what you want, show them your outline, and have them typeset everything. Then put a fancy border around the whole coupon and have it printed on colored paper. The best color of paper is a "dollar bill" shade of green. If you want to give it even more class, you could have it printed on green, lightweight card stock. You'll want to divide the "information" side of this coupon from the "business card" side with a dotted line and perforations.

If your layout this coupon properly. You should be able to get six of them on an eight and a half by one sheet of paper or card stock. This means the printer can print and cut six thousand of them for about the same cost as printing one thousand circulars or flyers.

There's also the idea of "just strolling through the park" on a Sunday afternoon. You take candid and interesting pictures of couples, children, and people in general, spending time with their relatives.

Keep tabs on the announcements of new births. Send advertising literature to the new mothers and follow up with phone calls, efforts to set up photography sessions.

Keep tabs on the engagement notices in the weekend papers. Send your sales literature to the brides-to-be and follow up with phone call efforts to take the wedding pictures.

Set up household and business photo inventory service. With this idea, you contact the insurance companies and determine if they will approve and endorse photographs you take of their policy holders' household, personal and business property in loss claims. Most will, and from there—working either with the help of an insurance agent, the agency itself, or on your own—contact owners of the property and sell them on the idea of your taking pictures of the household goods they have insured. You take pictures—a pictorial inventory of everything they're claiming or would like to claim on an insurance policy—and then identify the pictures, giving one set to the property owner and the other set to his insurance agent or company.

Picture inventories of household and personal property is still a new thing, but everywhere it's been introduced. It's definitely proven to be a super money maker for the people willing to get out and hustle.

If this idea arouses your interest, you might want to check into going franchise operation that gives you a complete business manual, operations guidebook, and ongoing consultation services: Photographic Inventory, PO Box 4046, Morgantown, West Virginia, 26505.

Once you decide that using your camera to generate extra income is what you're going to do, get out and use your camera, start taking pictures, and allow yourself the opportunity to build. Give yourself the chance and you'll quickly begin to think of hundreds of ideas for taking pictures, merchandising ideas for promoting your services, and sales angles for increasing your profits.

The important thing is to get started, regardless of how small your start, and begin chasing in on an idea that's still in its infancy. This is an idea that can produce new concepts for profit every day of the weak. An idea that can be fun as well as financially rewarding for you! You've got the idea and the plan, the rest is up to you. You've got the ball; now run with it.

On your printing, shop around for the best deal, but in the end, it shouldn't cost you more than about $60 for all six thousand coupons which will come from those one thousand sheets of paper or card stock.

Now, when you take a person's picture, regardless of whether it's an "in-store" setup, out on the golf course, or along the street, you give your customer one of your coupon receipts and tell them their prints will be ready in a couple of days. They fill in the information part of the coupon and give it back to you, retaining your "business card" portion of it.

When the prints are ready, you can phone the customer and remind him/her or volunteer to deliver and collect, send them through the mall with a bill, or make arrangements with a store to take care of them until the people call for them and pay at that time.

Most stores, golf courses, bowling centers, and other retail merchants will be glad to handle this part of it for you because it brings the customers back into the places of business and provides another sales opportunity for them. By all means, be sure to include an advertising circular with each set of pictures you deliver. This circular should explain how the customer can get more prints, how he can get enlargements of his favorites, and details relating to all the other photography services you offer.

Back to the original "in-store" picture firing set-up during evening shopping hours and on weekends for extra income. You can call attention to your "in-store" setup and bring in more business with a few merchandising promotional ideas. In the following paragraphs, we give the highlights of a few ideas that have worked well, however, you should keep your eyes open to observe additional promotional ideas that could be adapted to fit your new business.

Dress a helper in a down suit and take pictures of the kids on his lap or with his arm around the kids. Put a sandwich advertising board on a helper and let him stroll through the shopping center, advertising the fact that you're in a kiddie clothing store taking pictures.

Promote a "Baby of the Year" contest where you take pictures of babies, display the pictures on a "show board," and offer $100 cash plus a merchandise prize in a big drawing at the end of the year.

Set up a booth in the mall and promote "Instant Snapshots." Be a roving photographer and take candid shots of shoppers and promote a "Shopper of the Year" contest. Work with a clown and have him "attach himself to the kids" and ask if they'd like to have their pictures taken with him. Build an inexpensive and portable set, such as an airplane, a race car, bucking bronco, a hand-shaking scene with a famous person, or "balloon figures" and take pictures of people standing in or on these sets.

Get out to the golf course and take pictures of the golfers teeing off. Get over to the bowling centers and take candid shots of the bowlers in action. Do the same thing wherever there's a sports event taking place. Be on the spot and ready whenever there's an opportunity to take team pictures.

You might follow or hire someone else to follow a Little League team through its season, take candid and action shots. You then arrange the best of these pictures in a photo album with the team's name and year on the front. You should be able to sell one of these albums to each member of the team.

HOW TO MAKE BIG PROFITS IN MAIL ORDER STARTING FROM SCRATCH...

How to Make Big Profits in Mail Order Starting from Scratch

A lot of people are going to tell you that there are "no more secrets" to making the big profits in mail order. These same people will laugh at you and call you a "fool" for wasting your time chasing rainbows that don't exist... But don't you believe them or even listen to them! The opportunities for wealth beyond your wildest dreams—via the direct mail sales of a product or service—have never been greater!

If you have an idea—a product or service—now is the time to capitalize on it via mail-order selling. You can definitely start "on your kitchen table" and parlay it into millions of dollars... Others have done it, are doing it...and now, it's your turn for a piece of the pie.

As with any other profitable business, the procedure of making "profits" by mall has its own set of rules. Learn these rules, adhere to them, adjust them to your own circumstances—draw up a "battle plan" and work your plan... Persevere, be aware of other people's marketing methods, continue upgrading your own product or service, and with determination, you can become a millionaire in your own right... And then you can look over your shoulder at those who were laughing at you and perhaps help them in some small way...

Knowledge and the ability to use that knowledge are the basic keys to success. You must know what heights you want to attain, understand what it takes to attain those heights, and then dedicate yourself to getting there.

The rules to the achievement of success in direct mail success have to do with (1) market research, (2) the use of the "right" mailing lists, (3) customer follow-ups... If you can understand the "hows and whys" of these rules, then there's virtually no way you help but succeed in the field of mail order, even starting from scratch.

Market Research has to do with the selection of the proper product, identifying your "most-likely" buyers, and getting your product offer to these people.

Product selection is very basic and thus, the most important first step. Stop and think—look around yourself—and listen to what the "people" are clamoring most for...

In this day and age, much of the noise in the air has to do with: How can I find a job? How can I put together a resume that wins get me a job when I spot an opening? Where are the jobs? With these thoughts in mind, the person who writes, publishes, and gets an instructional manual or even a newsletter relative to these questions to the people will sell as many as he can produce...

So step one is to "listen" to what the people are wanting and then to satisfy those wants. You do this by spending some time researching the subject. Visit your local public library, interview a number of people involved who have succeeded in satisfying their wants, conduct a few "dry runs" for personal experience, and then write your manual. The "secret" to ultimate wealth is the capability of producing a product that can be duplicated an unlimited number of times for pennies and sold for dollars. A great many people get "bogged down" within this "rule" because they don't understand "time and motion" requirements.

As an example, if you were to stage seminars for the unemployed in your area to help them find and land jobs, you would undoubtedly make a fortune very quickly. But you would be committed to a certain expenditure of time every time you prepared for and staged a seminar. Thus, you would be making a lot of money for yourself, but at the same time, you'd sustain a loss of time to enjoy your wealth doing the things you always wanted to do once you became rich. The only way around this would be to train and hire other people to prepare for and stage the seminars which would mean you would then be dividing your profits.

At the bottom line then, the "only way" is to write something which can be duplicated as often as necessary and sold virtually forever. Look at it this way, you spend a full month organizing your material and writing a manual that costs you $1 per copy to produce in quantity. You sell it for $20 a copy, and over a period of three years, you sell three million copies—in essence, that amounts to $60,000,000 for one month's work!

So writing something "the people want" is the only way to go… But be careful… Make sure you've done your homework and what you write about is what the majority of the people "will stand in line to buy." Listen to what the people want and then give it to them… This is the product selection part of your market research… By listening to the cries for help and catering to them, you will not only have "discovered" the proper product, you will have also "identified" your buyers. Do not try to interest the people in something that does not specifically fulfill one of their wants. Don't mistake a casual interest or complaint as "the voice" of the masses. Spend some time "listening" and then write to satisfy what "the people" want.

Once you've got your product ready for customers to buy, you should spend some time creating the proper sales letter and/or circular you'll use in presenting it to your potential customers. Above all else, your sales materials must radiate an image of professionalism and sell, sell, sell…

Use quality paper and printing in presenting your sales message. Present what you have to say, not in a manner that tells the prospect who you are, how well qualified you are to write on the subject, or how much work you put into the project; but from a standpoint of how the customer is going to benefit from buying a copy of your manual

As an example, General Motors doesn't advertise cars by telling you how they were designed and engineered or built by college graduates or union workers nor have you ever heard of someone walking up to a car in a dealer's showroom, kicking the tire and exclaiming, "This sure looks like a safe one…" In fact, new cars are sold by the smell and the image of the prospective owner sitting in the driver's seat and showing off by driving through his neighborhood—just climb in there behind the wheel and see how she feels to you—go ahead and take it for a test drive, drive it home and see what your neighbors think. The benefits your prospective buyer is going to receive, that's the starting point from which all "winning" sales letters are written, circulars designed, and the "secret" of getting people to spend money on a product or service.

Students from the advertising classes at your local college, freelance advertising agency personnel, and, believe it or not, automobile dealership advertising managers are the people to turn to for ideas and help.

Next, is your follow-up piece. Ideally, this is a simple one-page listing of other "related" materials for your customers. So assuming you've sold him a manual on how to land a job, your follow-up piece might list manuals on how to dress to project a winning image, how to breeze through job interviews, and/or what to do after the interview perhaps! An opportunity for your buyer to subscribe to a quarterly newsletter listing job availabilities.

It's important that you have your follow-up piece put together and ready before you make your primary offer available to the public. Then when you start receiving orders, along with the manual the customer has ordered, simply also enclose your follow-up listing of other materials available. Thus, you make one sale and as a result of the first sale, you make further sales of related materials—the kind of "back-end" sales that will keep you in business and your profits multiplying. Don't neglect the follow-up piece.

Getting your offer to your most likely buyers is going to cost you money and here's where most direct mall beginners drop the ball. Do not try to save money and send your offer out to just any old list of names. Contact a reputable mailing list broker—visit your public library and ask the librarian for a copy of the standard rate of data services directory pertaining to mailing list brokers—tell the mailing list broker about your offer and ask for his help in choosing a mailing list that will be profitable for you. You'll probably have to rent a minimum of eight thousand names at a cost ranging between

$35 and $95 per thousand, but in the end, you'll save a lot of time and money because with a good offer and a good mailing list you count on a tremendous response. For instance, the one-time rental of a good mailing list may cost you $475 at $95 per thousand... But then, a 20 percent response from such a list on a $20 manual would mean $20,000 in your pocket.

To spend your time compiling names and addresses from incoming mail-order offers or to rent and use a mailing list from any source other than a reputable broker is not only foolish but a short-cut to the poor house! Identify your most-likely buyers, contact a reputable mailing list broker, match your "buyer profile" to his most responsive list, and you'll make money—lots of money—every time. Anything less is just an exercise futility!

There you have it, short and sweet, cut and dried, and the "easy way" to the big profits in mail order starting from scratch... These are the basics,—the secrets to how others have done it, and how you can do it too—organize yourself, follow these guidelines, and it'll be next to impossible for you not to succeed.

Remember though, your best product will be "how-to" information. Something the people "want" to learn. Something you can research, write about, and produce for pennies, and then sell for dollars. And don't forget, once you're ready to start taking orders, make sure that you get your offer to the most-likely buyers. Get out of the "mail-order circle" and to the people who want and will spend money for your product.

It's easy, it's simple, and it can be very rewarding! Understand the requirements, position yourself to succeed, and do it! This time next year, you could be a millionaire!

HOW TO START YOUR OWN DAY CARE CENTER

How to Start Your Own Day Care Center

There's a definite need for day care centers as more and more mothers of preschool-age children are forced to find jobs outside the home. This is due in part to the current economy and unfortunately, to the high divorce rate, which means mothers who might ordinarily stay at home and care for their own children, must seek income to help make ends meet.

Many experts expect the demand to increase through the turn of the century and the popularity of this type of business to continue growing from there. They base their forecasts on the fact that more and more young parents have happy memories of the time they spent in day care centers and title learning experiences they enjoyed. And again, there is the continuing need or desire of young mothers to work outside the home.

Profitable day care centers are much more than glorified babysitting services. Social researchers have found that the most important years in a child's development are those from one to six. Thus, the exposure to the world in which he lives, the instruction he receives, and the habits he forms during those years definitely affect his ability to learn and properly adjust as he progresses through his years of formal education.

For mothers of today—usually better educated than their mothers—are more aware of these factors and wanting the best for their children are demanding the structured preschool education and learning stimulation offered by modern day care centers. This is an honest desire of the mothers of preschool-age children, even those who aren't forced to work outside the home.

Another thing in your favor: even though there seems to be a trend for many large companies to finance and operate day care centers for their employees in or close by their factories or office buildings, studies show that most working parents prefer to leave their children closer to home than where they work. Thus, privately operated day care centers in residential neighborhood areas should not be worried too much about competition from the few company-operated day care centers.

The first step toward start-up of a profitable day care center is to understand what makes them profitable. There are a lot of day care centers operating with full enrollments of thirty-five to sixty-five children, but just barely breaking even. This is generally the result of regulations imposed by the state government, causing exorbitant overhead costs of operation. Basically, you'll need facilities to handle 150 to 200 children in order to realize annual profits in the "before taxes" bracket of $100,000.

Check with your state and local government regulatory agencies. Many states require day care centers to provide a minimum area per child, both inside and outside the building, plus at least one hot meal per day. A licensed teacher for every fifteen to twenty children and even a licensed nurse on the premises may be required. Be sure to know the regulations in your area and then design your business plan to meet these regulations.

Actually, you can begin by operating a babysitting service by learning and expanding from your profits and of course, through the long-term benefits of establishing a quality image. In fact, we recommend that you do start small—with a babysitting service—and build upon your progressive successes. Unless, of course, you have half a million dollars to invest.

Once you're beyond the babysitting stage, out of your home and backyard, beginning to build a real day care facility, you might try locating in your church or one of your area's civic club facilities. Also, you should check out the possibilities of renting or buying a vacant house. A large ranch-style home with a large backyard would probably suit your needs at this stage. But be sure you have zoning approval from your city council before signing a rent lease and finalizing your plans.

You might find, if you have your business plan in order, that a church or labor union will sponsor your business or even offer financial backing. Arranging some sort of partnership or sponsorship agreement with an established local organization will solve a lot of problems for you, not only in the area of space but in assistance with start-up costs and city father's approval.

Incidentally, a day care center is perhaps the ideal business for absentee ownership or a group of professional investors. Keep this fact in mind as you organize your plan and seek financing. See our business report, "How to Raise Money for Starting Your Own Business."

Generally, a "shoestring entrepreneur" in this business will do very well to locate in a vacant convenience store or even a vacant grocery store in a larger shopping center. The zoning will be in your favor, plus you'll have adequate parking space and less expense in partitioning or remodeling the building to suit your needs.

Ideally, your day care center should be located on a main thoroughfare with the building set back from the street. You should be on the right-hand side of the street as the traffic heads toward the major business or industrial areas of your community. In larger metropolitan areas, this would be on the city side of the "bedroom" communities. In smaller communities, you can locate just about anywhere except in the downtown area.

If at all possible, you should plan your facility similar to a hospital or motel entrance. This would be a driveway from the street to your door, usually under a covered drive-thru, with the driveway continuing back out to the street. Your long-term parking space would then be located in the center of the *U* or between the driveway and the street. You want to strive for the convenience of the parent in being able to drive right up to your door. She can drop off the child with only a few steps into your facility and easy access back onto the main thoroughfare.

Depending on your city sign ordinances and your finances, go all out with your sign. Advertise the name of your day care center, the hours you're open, whether you accept drop-ins, overnighters, or weekenders, and of course, your phone number. The sign makers and advertising people may strongly advise you against so much wording on your sign, but in this instance, don't listen to them. Your sign should state all essential information and serve to convince passersby that you can handle their childcare problems whenever the need arises.

If you initially locate in or through the sponsorship of a church or labor union, these people can assist you tremendously by including a mention of your services in their membership bulletins and bypassing out circulars or flyers.

You'll need to decide on your regular day care hours. Generally, these are from 6:00 a.m. through 6:00 p.m. You'll also need to decide whether you want to offer breakfast for the children. If so, you'll have to plan for a cook and food supplies for morning meals. We'll discuss kitchen facilities and kitchen help later, but the first decision must be if you will include breakfast. You'll already be set up with kitchen facilities and a cook because you will be serving a noon meal. If you do decide to offer breakfast for those parents not wanting to feed their children at home, you'll be able to add $8 to $12 per week to their billing. By buying your food supplies in bulk, you'll probably be able to realize some savings in overall food costs.

Mid-morning and mid-afternoon snacks are required in some states, but even where they're not required, they are pretty much standard fare in most day care centers. Fresh fruit, cookies, and juice are the usual snack foods served in most day care centers.

As mentioned earlier, you'll definitely be providing a hot meal for the children at noon. This entails a cook, dishes, planned menus, food supplies in bulk, and perhaps even small-sized tables and chairs. You'll also have to have kitchen help and facilities for washing the dishes.

These are just some of the important overhead costs you must plan for and of course, you will work to keep them as low as possible. As you should know by now, the greater your overhead, the more children you're going to have to take in and the more children you take in, the greater your space requirements.

All profitable day care centers operate according to planned routines. The day is broken down into one-hour segments with pre-planned curricula, much the same as classes at a public school. A typical day begins with a play period from whenever the children arrive until about nine o'clock. For this, you'll need indoor sandboxes, toys, and perhaps a family-sized television set. From nine to ten, the children are separated into groups—generally by ages—and you hold a reading or storytelling session. The mid-morning snack time is scheduled sometime between ten to eleven. For the younger children, this might include a mid-morning nap. After snack time, a learning session is usually held. Typically, this is the time when guests are invited in to speak or entertain the children.

Work with your Chamber of Commerce, civic clubs, and city administration for guests. Children will especially enjoy visits by policemen, firemen, and others who talk to them about citizenship, show films, and teach them about the things they do in the community. You can also get upperclassmen at your local colleges to visit and demonstrate such things as drawing, working with clay, building with wood, making things out of paper, and hundreds of other talents or skills they might be learning. The important thing is to bring "outsiders" in to talk to the kids about what goes on in their world.

Noon to one o'clock is generally lunch time, and from one until two is another learning session. During this afternoon learning session, you might offer the rudiments of reading, writing, and arithmetic. These teaching chores can be handled by college students studying to be teachers, retired teachers, or unemployed persons with teaching certificates. It's not so much a session to teach proficiency as a time to stimulate interest in formal education. The basic goal of most day care centers is to instill within each child a desire to learn more about the world in which he lives. Thus, each child should be full of plans for "when I get to be six years old and start school, I'm going to…"

About once a week, your afternoon learning session should be a tour or a trip to someplace that might be interesting as well as educational for the children. Again, you're making the idea of learning not only interesting but an exciting adventure as well. These trips can be anything from a walk in your immediate neighborhood to loading all the kids into cars or onto buses and taking them to the zoo. Check it out first, but on the whole, you'll find most businesses in your area will welcome opportunities to show the children around their offices or factories. The same thing quite naturally applies to your city offices, fire department, police department, and radio or television stations.

On days when you don't have a trip scheduled, your "learning session" might be a film or program related to nature, particularly animals. The advent of the video cassette recorder has opened endless possibilities in this area. Nap time and snack time will fill a period for younger ones, and books and quiet games will occupy older children who do not take a nap. When the nap period is over, they're allowed to play until their parents come by to pick them up.

Whenever possible, you should encourage the children to be outside during play periods. If you have lots of playground equipment, you won't necessarily always have to have organized games, but you will have to have a playground supervisor—someone to watch the children and see that they don't get hurt as they play. You can hire part-time help for this chore, perhaps from the local colleges, for minimum wage. If your city ordinances do not cover the specific age requirements of a playground supervisor, you might be able to hire students from your neighborhood high school. Select all the people you hire relative to their affinity with children and their dependability. Be aware of today's climate of extreme concern in protecting children in day care situations.

Your playground will require a fenced-in area. Drive around and look at the playground equipment in the play yard of your public schools and at day care centers in your area. You should have the basic sandboxes, swings, slides, and jungle gyms but in this area, you can be creative and original provided your equipment meets safety standards.

Some states require that you have a registered nurse on the premises, but generally, the main things needed are medical information from the parents and a written procedure to follow in case of accident or illness. Basically, when a child is injured or becomes ill, you should take him to the nearest medical center while another staff person gets in touch with the parents and explains what happened. If the parent cannot be present at the medical center, all information should be passed on to him/her immediately he/she is available.

It's a good idea to have all your helpers indoctrinated with basic Red Cross first aid knowledge and have a well-equipped first aid kit on the premises. As for any requirements relative to a full-time nurse, you should be able to hire registered nurses who are either not working or looking for extra income. You might be able to "hire the license" of a registered nurse. You pay a small fee to hang her license in your office, and she agrees to be available to serve your needs when you call.

Most day care centers are currently charging from $95 to $125 per child for a five-day week, plus $5 to $10 more for the inclusion of breakfast, with another $1.50 per meal when they serve an evening meal to the child. If you do not receive pay in advance, you can very quickly get "in the red." We strongly suggest setting up your financial structure and clients' payment schedules with this in mind. By having your customers pay in advance, you'll eliminate a lot of bookkeeping chores and time, the problems of collections, and you'll have operating funds with which to run the business. A point to stress when asking for payment by the month in advance is that because monthly payments are based on only four weeks of day care, they'll be getting a week of free service every three months.

Every profitable day care center requires a sharp manager or director. This person might be yourself or someone you hire for the job. Regardless, this person will be the key to your success. The director should have an empathy with people, be an excellent judge of people, be sales oriented, and have an outgoing personality. As much as anything else, this person must have the ability to listen to and really hear what other people are saying without the influence of preconceived opinions or making snap decisions. This person has to have the success of your business in mind at all times, which means building and mainlining an impeccable reputation.

Your director will be responsible for the hiring and supervision of your other help and the budgeting, scheduling, and overall day-to-day operation of the business. It is imperative to the success of your business that you have the very best person you can get in this position, regardless of the cost. A good director for a day care center will command a salary equal to teachers in your public schools, plus fringe benefit allowances such as free enrollment for their children and perhaps medical and dental insurance if you choose to provide group coverage.

When a prospective client calls to ask you about your services, you should explain how you operate and emphasize your invitation for them to bring their child in so that the two of them can be taken for a tour of your facilities.

Once in the center, your manager or director takes the parent and child on a tour, all the while explaining to the parent the advantages of the center's structured learning and play program as compared with everyday run-of-the-mill babysitting services, it's important to have the child along because as he sees the other children at play, he will be drawn to them and this will greatly influence the parent in deciding that your center is the right place for his or her child.

After the tour, steer the parent back into your administrative offices and propose enrollment of the child. Begin by asking where the parent works, what hours, and if he or she ever has to work overtime. You then ascertain the hours they'll want to drop off and pick up their child.

Strict procedures are absolutely essential regarding the pick-up of any child. Frightening as it may be to contemplate, we have all read accounts of strangers (or non-custodial parent) kidnapping a child. Printed forms must be provided and authorization signatures must be companied when anyone other than the legal guardian takes a child from your care. You will learn these requirements from your licensing office. Our advice to you is to follow them meticulously.

You should have a slickly printed, quality brochure showing your rates, your services, an outline of the curriculum, and a statement of your benefit goals for the children.

Check with a legally qualified person about the need for a contract. The parent will probably simply fill out a questionnaire file card giving address, place of employment, medical information about the child, and place he or she may be reached in case of emergency.

Most day care centers accept all children between two and six years of age. And there are many nowadays who take infants from six weeks. Of course, your personnel in this situation will be thoroughly oriented in infant care and you must ascertain if these babies are well when brought in to you. Otherwise, you put yourself in the position of "hospital" care instead of day care.

Generally, children aren't allowed to bring toys from home. You may want to allow the children to bring their own blanket from home for nap time, but if you allowed toys from home, you would be opening "Pandora's box" of possible problems relating to sharing and ownership. In light of this, you will want a full complement of appropriate toys and play items in your center.

If you decide to include short-term babysitting services, a good idea would be to include within the layout of your facilities a small one-bedroom apartment for a live-in person or couple. An older retired couple would be ideal with the husband serving also as maintenance and handyman.

Around-the-clock babysitting services, in addition to your regular day care center, can add tremendous and immediate cash-flow profits to your business, but correspondingly increase your payroll for qualified personnel. Such services would enable the parents to drop their children off in the evening and leave them around the clock or over the weekend. There will generally be no need for any planned program because these children will be sleeping during most of the time they're in your care.

As you establish the image and reputation of your day care center, the parents in your area will be much more inclined to leave their children with you for babysitting duties. And because you are considered tops in the area of responsibility, you'll be able to charge the very top rate of the babysitting fee structure. Keep current with fees charged by other quality businesses similar to yours.

The demand for unplanned or emergency babysitting services is very large. Not too many day care centers are aware of this potential for extra profits yet but the ones that are fine that their incomes can increase by 30 percent or more! We certainly recommend consideration of this idea for anyone involved in a day care service.

Another area that could mean enhanced profits for you is bus or van pickup service for the children. Of course, this would increase your operating costs (and consequently your fees), but the convenience of pickup is gaining in popularity. You'll need a custodian for indoor and outdoor cleanup and if you have access to a bus or van, he could be assigned additional duties as the driver. Some day care centers offering pickup service for their children contract with local transportation services to provide this service. Be certain of the driving experience of your driver if you contract for this transportation service.

Most day care centers open with very little fanfare or advertising. Generally, even without advertising, most are reporting 90 percent capacity enrollment within six months. With grand opening fanfare and a strong advertising campaign, you should be able to be at 90 percent capacity within your first six weeks. In an area where a severe shortage of day care facilities exists and with the right advertising and promotion, even sooner.

Your first step should be the door-to-door, handout distribution of a quality informative brochure. To save on costs, you can hire students attending advertising classes in your area colleges or even a freelance advertising copywriter to help you with the design and writing of this brochure. However, the bottom line should be that you have a good commercial printer do the printing on the best paper you can afford. All of this has to do with the image you're wanting to create and the quality of the service the "buyers" feel they're getting for the prices you are charging. Don't skimp on your brochure—you're aiming at people looking for the best place for their children.

You should place at least a two-column by four-inch grand opening display ad in your local newspapers. At the same time, you should place similar ads in the local magazines and other publications catering to the working mother. Send along a group picture of your staff and a story about your services with your advertising order. Phone the editors at your local newspapers, radio, and TV stations and invite them out to your grand opening. Be sure to place a "service information" ad in the yellow pages of your telephone directory. This should be the largest size you can afford. And remember that you need to make contact for a yellow page ad as well in advance of the release date of the directory.

After your grand opening and until you attain full capacity, continue to hand out your brochures at the entrances to the office buildings which house companies employing working mothers. Continue to run ads in your local newspaper, although these ads needn't be quite as large or run as regularly as the grand opening ads. Run an ad in the classified section describing your babysitting services.

At your grand opening, offer free refreshments for everyone. Coffee and punch for the adults with juice for the children and cockles for everyone. You should have members of your staff circulating among the parents to answer any questions and hand out brochures about the center.

You can begin small and expand in stages with your profits. However, you must draw up a long-range plan, detailing exactly what you intend to do and each milestone, you'll have to pass before proceeding to your next goal. In this way, you can succeed and attain not only the ultimate business but also the kind of profits planned at the start.

The basic and bottom-line secret to success with your own day care center will be your ability to hold your costs in line while achieving maximum capacity enrollment. You've got the plan, and my best wishes for success!

PARTY PLAN SALES
A Veritable Gold Mine For Wealth Builders

Direct Selling
Party Plan Sales

A veritable gold mine for wealth builders:

Believe it! You can easily make $50,000 in the next six months or less! After that, you can practically be guaranteed at least that much, but probably much more, every year for the rest of your life without really working!

The way to accumulate this kind of wealth is with your own business of selling merchandise via the party plan. Few other businesses can so easily give you this kind of wealth as quickly and keep your income growing.

A recent questionnaire circulated among hundreds of successful direct sales merchandisers across the country asked this question: "If you were to start over today, knowing what you know now and could choose the one method of merchandising that would make you really rich in the shortest period of time, which would you select?" Of these questionnaires returned, 94 percent stated they would go to the party plan method.

The sharp party plan operators (and the richest) simply hold motivational sales meetings for their sub-distributors about once a month. During these meetings, they are teaching their sub-distributors how to recruit new hosts and hostesses or husband and wife host and hostess teams. A host or hostess can be any person who is agreeable to holding a sales party at his or her house. Almost always, this person is rewarded for having the party with a percentage of the total business or an agreed-upon special merchandise gift. These people invite friends, neighbors, and relatives to the party. Your sub-distributor doesn't have to do much more than making contact with people willing to hold parties, supply the merchandise, and sometimes offer to help or be there to make sure everything goes smoothly.

Here's the kind of money you can realize with this business: Say you have ten sub-distributors and each one arranges only five parties a month and each party does $200 in gross business. That's a total of $10,000 per month in total volume. And from that total volume, you make only 30 percent. Figure it out for yourself. This would give you a personal income of $3,000 for thirty days in which you did no more than hold one or two motivational sales meetings!

Besides, each party is almost guaranteed to give your sub-distributor at least two more hostesses for future parties and those future parties will provide still more hostesses. This chain is endless and will build as fast as you can keep up with it.

To get your start in this fabulous method of merchandising, become a host or hostess yourself. Give a few parties yourself and learn the ropes. Choose an evening for your party—any evening except Friday through the weekend. Generally, 7:30 is the most convenient time for the greatest number of people. If it's inconvenient for whatever reason to hold a party in your home, arrange with a friend to hold the first couple of parties.

Make up a list of thirty to sixty people you can invite to the party. They can be friends, neighbors, relatives, or people you know from work, even acquaintances with whom you do business such as the checkout clerk where you buy your groceries or people you meet at the bus stop on your way to work.

After formally inviting these people, you then call to remind them of the party at least a couple of days before the date of the party. This is important because of the original forty people you invite, at least eighteen will not show because it slipped their minds, last-minute circumstances that force a change in plans, and those that really weren't interested in the first place.

On the day of the party, get your merchandise display set up early. The party should be held in the largest room in the home—usually the living room—with the merchandise display the center of attraction. The merchandise should be set out on a sturdy table covered with a good white or light-colored cloth, and the merchandise should be arranged by group or type—the jewelry items together; perfumes, bath oils and colognes together; crystals together, and so on. Try to put a bit of imagination and showmanship into your merchandise display. This will have the effect of making your merchandise look much more valuable than it actually is. Those that do put a flair into their merchandise displays find that it increases their sales by as much as 25 percent over an ordinary showing. For instance, a high-intensity light focused on the display will cause the jewelry to sparkle, the stainless steel to gleam, and the brassware to glimmer like valuable heirlooms.

Another idea would be to tack a piece of velvet onto a four-by-six-foot piece of plywood and use it to display rings, earrings, necklaces, and watches. In jewelry sales, another idea is to hang a mirror on a wall near the merchandise display. If you or your hostess has room, you might want to set up a card table covered with an expensive-looking piece of material. Place a dressing table-type mirror on this table with a chair available for your guests to sit at the table while they try on the various items. The guests then make their selections after determining how each item looks on them.

Regardless of what you do to make it easier for your guests to select and buy, a hand mirror is an absolute must whenever you're showing jewelry. It would be wise to have several hand mirrors available—two for your merchandise display table and an extra one on the "admiration" table.

Besides your merchandise display, be sure also you're organized with your refreshments. These usually consist of coffee, tea, soft drinks, cookies, or other "nibble" items. The host or hostess usually makes arrangements in advance for one of the guests to assist with the serving of refreshments.

Be sure you have name tags for your guests and a couple of felt-tip marking pens. And don't forget the order forms. These should be standard two-piece self-carbon order forms—one copy for your customer and the other for your files. The best idea is to buy the order forms. All these items are commonly available in stationery stores. Rubber-stamp your name and address on each copy of each order form, at least a couple of days in advance of the party.

Still another item to remember is your merchandise catalogs. Be sure you have a good supply on hand, rubber stamped with your name and address. Later on, when you're established and the money is rolling in, you can have your name and address imprinted on the catalogs.

If you don't have a merchandise catalog, consider making one of your own.

While we're on the idea of catalogs, we'd like to point out that a lot of party plan merchandisers are also dealers for the extra-income book catalog, *Unique Books*. They feel that almost everyone is interested in extra-income ideas and the *Unique Books* catalog has a wide selection of reports and manuals describing supplemental income opportunities. Leaving one of the book catalogs with guests at the party results in an ongoing flow of book orders for months afterward.

Back to the party plan. About a half hour before your guests are due to begin arriving, turn on all the lights in the room where the party is to be held. This will give the room a bright, warm feeling conducive to a party kind of atmosphere. And by all means, be sure to turn off all the radios, stereo, and TV sets. Eliminate any and all noises from other rooms in your home that might distract the attention of your guests.

Every party should be planned and follow a prescribed format or agenda. This is because, without a plan, it will just be a gathering of people wasting time at your home instead of theirs. You must have a plan to know what to do next in order to achieve the desired results. Having a "pattern" is also the easiest way to teach others to duplicate your success and the idea of following a successful formula is a proven method of making the most sales in the least time.

Phase one is the greeting and get-acquainted time slot—about thirty minutes. The hostess greets the guests as they arrive, prints a name tag for each, introduces them around, gives them a catalog, points out the refreshments, and leads them into conversation with the other guests.

The second phase is the "game-playing" portion of your part. This phase is used to relax everybody and get them involved in the party. It should last about fifteen to twenty minutes.

Next comes the merchandise presentation by the hostess, who shows and describes each item on display. If you have jewelry available, ask different guests to try on particular items and show the others what these articles look like in use. The length of time spent on this phase of the party will depend in a large part on how much merchandise you have on display, but generally, you shouldn't spend more than about twenty minutes showing and describing your merchandise. Then give your guests about ten to fifteen minutes to personally inspect and try on the items that have aroused their interest.

You should mingle and converse with the guests during this time period in order to answer specific questions or explain the possible uses of an item, where it might look good in the buyer's home, and any interesting tidbits relating to where an item came from, how it was made, or the satisfaction of an earlier buyer. When you seem to have answered all the questions, and everyone appears to have made their selections, start writing orders. Don't hesitate to ask for orders. Writing orders should take about fifteen minutes and then you should let the party begin to winding down.

During this time, mingle with your guests and anyone showing a spark of interest should be approached with an offer to serve as a future host or hostess. As each guest starts to leave, thank them for coming and walk with them to the door.

The total length of your party shouldn't be much more than two hours. Time and time again, it's been proven that you can do everything necessary and make the most sales in this period of time. You lose effectiveness and make fewer sales with appreciably more or less time.

There are a couple of proven ways to recruit new hosts or hostesses from the people attending your party. First of all, watch the guests as they look over the merchandise, examine, admire, and wish for something they don't quite have enough extra money to buy. When you've determined that a particular guest wants a specific item but can't quite fit it into the budget, simply take her aside to a secluded corner of the room and explain privately that you're willing to give her the item she has been looking at and wanting if she will agree to invite her friends and relatives to a party in her home. This approach works almost every time, and your only expense is the wholesale price of the item you give her as a free gift.

The second surefire approach is to offer a cash incentive. You do this by offering to allow 5 percent to 10 percent of the total sales volume resulting from the party staged for you by this type of new recruit. There's a plus factor for you on this one because you'll be getting the enthusiastic participation of the host or hostess on the selling side. Once you've explained to them how your program works, they'll generally do everything they can to make the party a huge success and thereby increase their pay for the evening.

When you give a gift to the hostess for having the party, the presentation should be a special ceremony staged with all the "showbiz" flair you can muster at the end of your merchandise showing. However, when your gift is a cash award, carry your presentation over to the next party and make a big production of it as well. Don't forget to invite the "guest of honor" to your next scheduled party for the big presentation. During these presentations, many of the other guests will be favorably impressed and as a consequence, will ask you for details.

Actually, your recruiting efforts should begin when you start taking orders. Every person you talk with should be offered the opportunity to hold a party of his or her own. Then just before the party begins breaking up, ask your guests as a group if any of them would be interested in holding a similar party in his or her home. You ask those who voice an interest to stay over for a few minutes in order to work out the details. You should have an appointment book for this scheduling. Simply ask what date would be favorable for them, mark that date in the book, along with the name, address, and telephone number. Then assure each that you'll call in the next day or two to work out the details.

Many party plan merchandisers also use a letter. They write a letter extolling the fun and excitement of the parties, explaining briefly the opportunities to receive free gifts of their choice or big commission checks. Then they invite the letter recipients to call for complete details on how they can stage a party. These letters are usually printed in volume and then slipped inside the covers of the catalog these merchandisers give to each person attending the parties. Sometimes these letters are handed to each guest as the party breaks up.

Some party plan merchandisers also run small classified ads in the area newspapers. Their advertising plays up the opportunities available to make regular commission checks (extra income) simply by holding parties in their homes. People interested are invited to phone for more details. Response to this kind of ad is generally very good with the conversion rate better than 60 percent!

Most people tend to feel party plan merchandising is exclusive to women, but don't you believe it! It's true that women generally establish themselves more rapidly than men with this kind of sales operation, but over the long haul, there are just as many men operating successful party plan sales operations as there are women. Men are usually not as adept at establishing social "chitchat" relationships as women. Therefore, the man who wants in on the vast potential of party plan merchandising should consider working with a woman.

A husband-and-wife partnership is an ideal working arrangement. An acquaintance, girlfriend, or relative will often work out just as successfully. The basic requirement is simply that the "couple" must function as a team with the individual talents of one complementing those of the other. Probably one of the greatest secrets of success with this kind of sales operation is that in order to make the sales and talk about $400 parties, you must have the widest selection of merchandise possible.

Many beginners, not understanding that offering the potential buyers a wide and varied selection of items to choose from is what builds your profits in a hurry, base their entire merchandising plan around a selection that's of special interest or particularly appealing to themselves. It's all right to include the items that you especially like, but don't base your entire merchandise line on the things you like; you're selling to others, not yourself!

Most successful party plan merchandisers advise that you should display at least forty different items and more if you have the supplier contacts or the buying expertise. The actual decisions on which products to carry and display at your parties should be based upon these four factors:

1) The kinds of gift items, personal decor articles, and general merchandise the people in your area are buying
2) The styles or fads currently in vogue in your area
3) Contacts with enough suppliers who can furnish you with the kind of merchandise your potential buyers want
4) Your ability to shop among the various suppliers and verify that you are getting the very best merchandise value obtainable.

Still, another important point to consider before buying merchandise to display and sell: Do the prices you're having to pay for your products wholesale allow you enough room for a reasonable profit when compared to your time and expense?

Do some market research relative to your ambitions; get answers to the questions we've set forth for you and when you're satisfied that you understand the workings of party plan merchandising, grab the opportunity and run with it!

About the Author

Dear reader,

My name is Jeffrey Crockett a college graduate that majored in health and physical education and a completion of a Master's program in special education courses with three credits toward a doctoral degree. In my endeavor to rise out of student loan debt, my purpose is to show you different ways how to earn money from home and introduce a positive contribution to your neighborhoods, communities, and society yet strive toward financial independence.

www.ingramcontent.com/pod-product-compliance
Lightning Source LLC
Chambersburg PA
CBHW040519220526
45473CB00012B/2911